There are a multitude of different immigration petitions and applications. They are complex and full of requirements. Obviously it would be best to hire an immigration attorney to best prepare the petitions and applications. However, this can certainly cost thousands of dollars.

The next best option is to get a sample of the petition written by an experienced immigration attorney. The samples cost a fraction what would be charged by an immigration attorney. However, while the reader has to alter, amend and change the parts of the sample petition to reflect their actual situation, it is a fantastic roadmap for them to use. If the reader has purchased the entire petition or application, they will have real live samples of cover letters, forms, declarations, affidavits and the necessary exhibits to use. The samples come from real cases and the names of those clients have been redacted to protect the privacy of that person or corporation.

These are petitions and applications that have been drafted by an experienced immigration attorney with over 25 years of experience. Get the benefits of that experience without the costs.

ATTORNEY DRAFTED IMMIGRATION PETITIONS

By

Brian D. Lerner
Attorney at Law

The Law offices of Brian D. Lerner, APC. The law practice consists of Immigration and Nationality Law and everything involved with and regarding immigration which includes citizenship, investment visas, family and employment visas, removal and deportation hearings, appeals, waivers, adjustment, consulate processing and all types of immigration and citizenship matters. Thousands of families have been reunited and/or permitted to stay in the U.S. and/or return to the U.S. because of the successful work of Immigration Attorney Brian D. Lerner.

This law offices handles all types of immigration cases including family based and employment based. Immigration issues range from immigration court proceedings to trying to fix what paralegals may have done that was neither correct nor proper. Foreign nationals must have experience lawyers admitted to practice law.

The Law Offices of Brian D. Lerner, APC, handles cases arising from business visas, work permits, Green Cards, non-immigrant visas, deportation, citizenship, appeals and all areas of immigration. The Law Offices of Brian D. Lerner, APC does EB-5 Investor Visas, H-1B Specialty Occupation, L-1 Intracompany Transferee, E-2 Treaty Investor, E-1 Treaty Trader, O-1 Extraordinary Ability among others. Regarding immigrant visas for the Green Card, the firm does PERM and advanced degree PERM, Family Petitions, and Extraordinary Alien Petitions. In addition to affirmative petitions, the Law Firm represents people in people in deportation and removal hearings, including political asylum, withholding of removal, and convention against torture cases.

Brian D. Lerner has been certified as an expert in Immigration & Nationality Law by the California State Bar, Board of Legal Specialization since 2000 and has been recertified three times. He now passes on his decades of experience by allowing the Reader, Law Schools, Professors and other Immigration Attorneys to purchase sample petitions on every facet of Immigration Law.

TABLE OF CONTENTS

ABOUT THE BUSINESS PLAN GUIDE

This sample Business Plan has been prepared by an Immigration Lawyer with over 25 years of experience. You will get the hard copy as well as an thumbdrive with the loaded PDF. There are charts, graphs, and market segments for exactly what the U.S. Consulate is looking for with your Business Visa Application. Whether it is an E-2 Treaty Investor Visa or L-1 Intracompany Transferee Visa, you can save thousands by using this Business Plan and altering it to your specifications.

Sample Business Plan for L-1 and E-2

Table of Contents

Executive Summary

Opportunity

Problem

Newberry, Florida is a thriving community of educated residents, ambitious students and established corporates. It has a supportive governing body which promotes not just business expansion in the state but also a thriving arts and culture community.

Serving as an employment and retail hub for Alachua County and 11 surrounding counties, and as home to the University of Florida and Santa Fe College, the city of **Newberry is the region's economic, cultural and educational nucleus**.

Due to this, there is a **high need for a boutique studio** which can capture the rich life its residents live, in terms of memorable moments, cultural events and closed group functions. Similarly, corporates need help showcasing their best value proposition to their customers, to enable better business growth. The current players in this space are unable to meet the demands of high quality, integrated, and technologically advanced work which will provide its residents a superior way of capturing their memories and corporates to grow their business.

These include high quality photography &/or videos produced as per their requirements; be it for an event, or a marketing campaign, or website creation or even instructional videos.

Solution

We see immense opportunities in these areas of personalized and customized photoshoots – all at once place, in the heart of Newberry!

The ▓▓▓▓▓▓▓▓ provides all types of photography and video solutions, including, and not limited to:

- Special event

- Marketing requirements
- In Studio or outside photoshoots
- Glamour Portrait photography
- Architectural photography and aerial 3D photography
- Audio Video capture of special events, cinematographic style.
- Audio Video post production
- Instructional videos for companies/institutions

Our unique selling proposition will be creativity with contemporary sensibilities, high aesthetics, superior technological quality and premium end to end solutions for the customer - all this at reasonable pricing. We plan to target mainly high net worth individuals and small and medium corporates in and around Newberry.

Our President, Mr. James Fernandez, is highly talented, creative, resourceful and an acclaimed photographer, with more than 20 years of experience. Over the years, he has perfected the art of creative photo-shoots, gaining valuable in-depth knowledge of the nuances of the profession.

Market

Our market research indicates a targeted market size of approx. $68 million per annum - our focus for the next 2-3 years is to capture at least 1% of that space.

Our business plan projections promises break-even in the first year with sales of $375,000 and a healthy profit margin of 25%.

We are targeting three core groups:

1) High networth individual portfolios (40%)

2) Corporate videos (40%)

3) Tourists, visitors and residents (20%)

Competition

We see great scope in the services that we are offering, with only a handful of firms in and around Newberry, Florida providing the creativity and resources on par with ours.

We have identified some of our potential competitors in Newberry, namely:

- Drones Unlimited: http://www.dronesunltd.com/
- Aerial Drone Solution: http://www.aerialdronesolutions.info/
- Mike Shea Photography: http://www.mikeshea-photo.com/
- Cheuvront Studios: http://www.cheuvront.com/

We do understand that customers might choose from them due to ongoing personal relationships.

Why Us?

We plan to differentiate ourselves from them using the below strategies:

1. **Creativity with Contemporary Style**
2. **Premium Customer Service with Integrated Solutions**
3. **Superior Quality with High Technological Expertise**
4. **President's Experience**

What we will offer is state of the art, and addresses the problem statement - imagine, having an immersive video made, that allows you to recreate that special moment all over again, as though you were there once more!

The current market needs a creative studio who can provide holistic end to end customized solutions for these needs. Hence, we see a great market opportunity here for our core services.

Expectations

Forecast

This falls under 3 main categories:

1. **Tourists & High Net worth Individuals:** Studies indicate that Florida is home to multiple events, year-round. All of these festivals are practically year round activities, and confirmed crowd pullers. At these activities, families and individuals come to have a great time, create special memories, celebrate occasions and, overall, have a great experience. Photographs and videos are the need of the moment from everyone, for them to capture this experience of their memories. Especially, in a manner which captures what they saw, felt and thought, while they were participating in those events.
2. **Students & Residents:** Residents have a strong thriving community, with art and culture being a very strong part of their life. They have a need to capture their memories in an aesthetic manner, including personal close group events as well such as weddings and graduations.
3. **Corporates:** Newberry has a strong and growing corporate presence which need good storytelling experts to tell and market their stories to their potential customers. This ranges from technological support such as website design to content creation such as advertisement videos, instructional clips etc.

Corporate and individuals desire photography and videography options that are convenient, unique and produce breathtaking results, in a manner that is quick and of high-quality service.

Financial Highlights by Year

Financing Needed

The initial seed money for the capital investment on equipment and for running the operations in the initial stages comes from our parent firm in Argentia, San Juan Cinema Ltda.

San Juan Cinema Ltda. has already invested more than $28,000 in USA towards equipment and premises rentals.

Opportunity

Problem & Solution

Problem Worth Solving

About Newberry

The Newberry MSA was ranked as the No. 1 place to live in North America in the 2007 edition of 'Cities Ranked and Rated'. Newberry was also ranked as one of the "best places to live and play" in the United States by National Geographic Adventure in the same year.

Highlights of Newberry:

- 1,169,000 residents, including Alachua County and 11 surrounding counties.
- Nearly 75,000 college students
- Greater Newberry is the state's youngest and most educated region (18 to 44 year-olds and people with advanced degrees)
- 4th best tax climate in the nation for businesses and residents
- State GDP ranks 19th in the world

Attractive place for Corporates

As a base for several small, medium & large corporate firms, Newberry has strong infrastructure for businesses across sectors. There are multiple reasons for this, being:

1. Low cost of doing business
2. Diverse, highly educated talent pool
3. Access to research, innovation and technology through leading faculty members
4. Supportive environment for industry and startups
5. Technology-focused incentives
6. Talent available across the education spectrum

Source: http://www.gainesvillechamber.com/economic-development/https://en.wikipedia.org/wiki/Newberry,_Florida

Newberry as a Hub of Arts & Culture

Newberry is known as a strong supporter of the visual arts. Each year, two large art festivals attract artists and visitors from all over the southeastern United States. Cultural facilities include the Florida Museum of Natural History, Harn Museum of Art, the Hippodrome State Theatre, and the Curtis M. Phillips Center for the Performing Arts. Smaller theaters include the Acrosstown Repertory Theatre (ART), Actors' Warehouse, and the Newberry Community Playhouse (GCP). GCP is the oldest community theater group in Florida.

The presence of a major university enhances the city's opportunities for cultural lifestyles. The University of Florida College of the Arts is the umbrella college for the School of Music, School of Theatre and Dance, School of Art and Art History, and a number of other programs and centers including The University Galleries, the Center for World Art, and Digital Worlds.

Newberry is well known for its music scene and has spawned a number of bands and musicians.

- The Spring Arts Festival, hosted each year, usually in early April, by Santa Fe College (formerly Santa Fe Community College), is one of the three largest annual events in Newberry and is known for its high quality, unique artwork.
- The nationally recognized The Downtown Festival and Art Show, hosted each fall by the City of Newberry, attracts award-winning artists and draws a crowd of more than 100,000
- The Hoggetowne Medieval Faire has attracted thousands of fairgoers for over 20 years
- The Newberry Improv Festival provides a venue for new talent
- The Fest, a multi-day, multiple-venue underground music festival that has been held annually in Newberry, FL since 2002

Our Solution

From our study of the market, customers, existing players and our core experience, our business proposal is for a *premium specialized integrated creative arts studio* to create exquisite audio visual stories for individuals and corporate brands (small & medium size), which bring alive their uniqueness.

Unique Selling Proposition:

- High quality creative rendition of content, using state of art audio visual technology
- Delivered at a one-stop shop, in an end to end integrated solution, thereby delighting the customer

The ████████ will provide all types of photography and video solutions, including but not limited to:

- **Still Photography:**

1. Indoor Theme Studio Still Shoot
2. Outdoor Themed Photoshoots
3. Portfolio Creation: Glamour Portrait Photography for events, aspiring models
4. Architecture Photography: Including aerial 3D photography (Drone Photography) for real estate customers as well as businesses/factories

- **Videography:**

1. Event Coverage using audio visual medium – capturing it in cinematographic storytelling style (For example graduations, weddings)
2. Post production and editing work.

- **Marketing Content Creation**

1. End to end website designs
2. Architectural photography and aerial 3D photography
3. Instructional videos for companies / institutions who need to show how their services work, products functions, company orientation, culture change videos. etc.

- **Equipment Rental**

1. Rent out high cost equipment to other service providers only if they are idle, to generate a supplementary source of cash and optimize the use of photo shoot equipment
2. Done through third party operators.

- **Ancillary Services**

1. Associated services like printing and framing services to ensure end to end experience for the customer

Target Market

Based on our extensive market research, we have found that residents and tourists in Newberry find it difficult to have high quality photographs &/or videos produced as per their requirements, in a manner that suits their purpose.

Similarly, corporates who aspire to grow their business further through marketing campaigns, website creations or even instructional videos, find it difficult to identify capable, creative and professional service providers who can partner with them.

This is because the market currently is not being served adequately with the existing service providers. Compounding the matter is the lack of creative, professional, technologically inclined and accessible professionals who can do all of this - at one place.

Hence there is a need of an integrated solutions provider who can provide these high quality and value added services at a reasonable cost, with a potential market size of approx. $68 million.

Key Clientele Contribution to Revenue:

- **High net worth residents:** Our focus here is on the boutique personalized kind of work which will meet unique needs of high net worth individuals. We envisage this to contribute about 40% to our revenue. Examples of there are:

1. A couple requesting us to film the story of their life
2. Portrait Photography, such as parents who want to capture their graduating students, people about to get married, etc.

- **Corporates (Small & Medium):** Work with corporates to meet their needs for external and internal marketing. We forecast that this will contribute about 40% to our revenue. Sample set of these are:

1. Big factories or businesses that want to improve their web presence by high quality architectural and interior photography.
2. Architectural photography - real estate agents who need to improve the quality of their sales pitch by high quality pictures and 3D aerial shots
3. Other key examples are advertisements, instructional videos, employer brand videos, training videos.
4. Local businesses who hire part time students to clean houses and businesses - their website is outdated with pictures that don't reflect well what they do. They are already interested in hiring us to showcase their value proposition better.

- **Tourists & Students:** We will meet retail needs of residents by primarily using a quick, replicable model. For example, a wedding photo book. We estimate this category would contribute about 20% of our revenue.

Competition

Current Alternatives

The market study has revealed that some of our direct competitors in Newberry are:

Drones Unlimited

Aerial Drone Solution

Mike Shea Photography

Gainesville360

Cheuvront Studios

They each offer a customized solution to their clients as well; and we understand that customers might choose them for their long-established presence in the market and one-to-one contact with residents.

Our Advantages

What we will offer is state of the art, and addresses the problem statement - imagine, having an immersive video made, that allows you to recreate that special moment all over again, as though you were there once more!

The demand currently is not being met through existing players as none of them specialize in delivering an integrated service, despite its clear popularity in other nearby and similarly sized cities. Lack of affordable and 'all-in-one' local studio is also a common complaint, especially those from the region itself who are looking for an exquisitely crafted reminder of events.

We plan to differentiate ourselves from them using the below strategies:

- **Creativity with Contemporary Style**
- **Premium Customer Service with Integrated Solutions**
- **Superior Quality with High Technological Expertise**
- **President's Experience**

These factors have been explained in detail below:

- **Creativity with Contemporary Style:**
    1. Our aesthetic sensibility is modern and fresh. What we offer is a state of the art design sense, which will address the consumer need with a high degree of imagination to create the final product.
    2. This will be supported by newer ideas such as drone video filming which gives a fresh way to demonstrating creativity
- **Premium Customer Service & Integrated Solutions:** From consultation to photo-shoots to delivery, we will be at the customer's service and deliver in the fastest time possible - all from one place.

    1. For example, we can provide a real estate company with exterior and interior photos of their properties, as well as aerial photo or videos from a height. Our competitors are usually only doing one or the other, not both. Similarly, for glamour portrait photography, we can do both in studio or outdoors. Lastly, if somebody else shot a video and needs it edited, color corrected, etc., we can provide our services to them.

- **Superior Quality with High Technological Expertise:** For all the services we offer, we can go beyond the standard capturing and editing of images, but also aid in publishing them online on websites by using digital technology to serve our customers better.

1. This requires high technical understanding to ensure the audio visual work is platform agnostic and is showcased in the best manner regardless of the platform. This gives us the freedom to handle big clients and complex projects, which the current competitors are unable to do.
2. With an in-depth knowledge of "resolutions", "frame rates", and other technical specifications – our President has delivered 'miracles' for clients who demand that certain 'extra' in their event photography, quickly and easily and at a price that is highly cost-effective
3. As a measure of our maturity in this segment, we are moving away from the traditional SLR and DSLR cameras to Mirrorless cameras that will enable superior quality

- **President's Experience:** Mr. James Fernandez is hugely talented, creative, and resourceful; not just in running businesses but also in audio visual arts. He has more than 20 years of experience and has extensive experience in conceptualizing the best way to showcase a client's script or story, guiding the narrative and directing its creative as well as technical aspects, in a manner that fulfils the vision.

1. Has exceptional artistic vision and creative skills, in addition to having an extensive understanding of the filmmaking process
2. A hands-on director and can handle video & photo editing, technical equipment, camera-work and other supporting activities with comfort
3. An experienced producer with having produced more than 100 hours of content for diverse projects spanning television and movies
4. Started independently managing businesses at 26 years of age. Has led and grew business in audio visual media space, property development to generate an average revenue of ~ $80,000 per annum using strong people skills, analytics & business acumen.

Given the above reasons, we feel certain of making a strong presence in this market in the next 1-3 years.

Execution

Marketing & Sales

Marketing Plan

Our key marketing strategies and plan to ensure business growth and to attract the right quality of customers are:

- **Right Pricing:** We based our product pricing on a close study of all of our competitors in the downtown and campus areas. Our prices should be 'on par' with competitors in the first year, and based on volume and customer feedback we will modify it depending on the market understanding. A tentative first year price model is shown below:
    1. $200-$500 Portraits
    2. $300-$800 Aerial shots
    3. $200-$500 Interior Architectural Photoshoots
    4. $1,000 to $4.000 Video or Photo Production for web, television
    5. $40-$80/hour Editing
    6. $100-$300 Printing/Framing

- **Use Search Engine Optimization:** Our primary competitive advantage would be to ensure **our firm is the first search engine result** if anybody searches for terms such as "event photography Newberry"/ (North Florida) / "drone photography"/ "video editing"/ "post production help" and for other services which we provide
    1. This will be free of cost to us, hence saving money spent on advertisements. Our President is an expert on SEO and can do this without paying anything extra
    2. This will help us gain new clients on a fast pace
    3. This will ensure serious clients who are already looking for this effort, hence saving us the effort to market and 'push' our firm with separate advertising

- **Strong Digital Presence:** We will leverage our website to be ready and compatible with all platforms including mobile devices and use that to enable:
  1. Online booking
  2. Providing information about our services
  3. Incorporate videos and photos that showcase our products and capabilities
  4. Showcasing testimonial and delivery standards
- **Direct Marketing:**

  1. We will have an email signup form on our website
  2. We will be featured in the local marketing of a popular magazine, and will test a local service that hands out coupons on the streets downtown, in the lobbies of several key office buildings, University of Florida campus and major tourist destinations of Newberry

- **Social Media Marketing:** We will leverage social media to reach out to appropriate audience such as students

Sales Plan

Selling Strategy: As detailed out earlier, our strategy will be to get the customer base who wants better quality and experience, and hence is willing to pay premium for it. The core sales process will leverage our aesthetic sensibilities, ability to capture nuances, innovative angles of shooting, master storytelling in capturing the content and the ability to provide end to end solutions.

In the initial business phase, the President will be himself, focusing on sales. In the second year onwards, once the core customer base is set, he will be supported by another employee.

We are confident of at least 14 customers per week from the various target groups identified, with an estimated revenue of approx. $375,000 in the first year.

Payment Method: Our business will be equipped for any interface running the point-of-sale apps. Furthermore, we will be in a position to accept payments by Visa,

MasterCard, American Express, Apple Pay, Bitcoin and PayPal. We also have a small till at the retail outlet to accept cash payments and make change

Operations

Locations & Facilities

We will operate out of a commercially zoned, rental premises. We recently signed a one-year lease on the premises, located only 7 minutes drive from the University of Florida. We envisage operating The ▮▮▮▮▮▮▮▮ 7 days a week.

The premises is excellent and ideal for our profession as it is:

· Attractive & safe: The location is a popular entertainment space and is conveniently located in a safe neighborhood near both the downtown district and the university; making it easy for us to attract customers from both of those areas.

· Easy for customers: With ample parking place, thereby saving the customer time and making it easy for customers to visit us without thinking about challenges of parking.

Basis customer feedback, we plan to expand our office in our second or third year to enhance ambience and our service standards. The aim is that although we are based in Newberry, we can serve all of North Florida / South Georgia, and subsequently, any location across the world.

Technology

Below are the key web based tools we will use to run operations efficiently.

- **Marketing:** MailChimp to send email newsletters, and the usual social media sites (Facebook, Instagram, etc.) to connect with our customers and solicit feedback.
- **Payment & Delivery:** A multi-platform app, which we will use to accept credit card payments, make bookings, integrate with local delivery services and to

enable customers to sign up for our email newsletter using the MailChimp Subscribe app

- Accounting: QuickBooks Online

Equipment & Tools

We have numerous units of high end photography and videography equipment. These include professional cameras and lenses, lighting equipment, drones, large format printers, editing software / hardware, besides accessories. We have procured this and have the funds to procure more based on demand.

We have so far invested about $28,000 in the equipment and will most likely invest another $10,000 as we commence operations. The break up of this is:

- Original investments: $42,995
  - $28,862 in Photo/Video Gear
  - $1,000 in starting up costs
  - $415 rent/month for the space and facility.
- Remaining Operation Budget Available before sales: $10,000 for new gear

Milestones & Metrics

Milestones Table

Milestone	Due Date
Finalize Business Plan	June 30, 2017
Submit L-1 Application	July 15, 2017
Launch Local Marketing & Advertisement, including SEO	August 05, 2017
Create Website	August 15, 2017
Begin Operations and Hiring	August 31, 2017

Company

Overview

San Juan Cinema Ltda. is in the business of renting its own 6 fully furnished apartments to foreigners, expats and tourists that are in need of short and long term rentals with zero hassles.

It started in 2009 as Cinema Argentia Ltda and was an audiovisual production company with its primary focus on high end video and photo equipment rentals, video production and editing. In 2013 the company changed its name to "San Juan Cinema Ltda." since it closed the audiovisual part of business and invested in real estate. This enabled the President to manage long distance remote administration as he moved to US due to spouse's study requirements.

Team

Management Team

James Fernandez, President of The ▮▮▮▮▮▮▮ is an entrepreneur with more than 20 years of experience in starting, owning and running businesses. Mr. Fernandez has a deep knowledge and passion for filmmaking and his key experience has been in the areas of photography, film direction and video editing, where he has provided end-to-end solutions to clients.

His key skills lies in the area of Storytelling, Photography & Film Direction and audio visual content production. He has rich experience in conceptualizing the best way to showcase a client's script or story, guiding the narrative and directing it's creative as well as the technical aspects to achieve fulfillment of the vision.

He is an accomplished photographer and videographer. His firm in Argentia, San Juan Cinema Ltda (formerly Cinema Argentia Ltda.), had successfully provided this service in Argentia for more than eight years, with a pause since the last four years as he had other personal endeavors here in USA.

We plan to strengthen our team gradually, as the business grows. Initially, we are going to start with our President managing the starting phase activities himself. As we establish the business, our strategy will be to outsource all jobs except the aspects where we add value to our customers such as design, conceptualization, technology, customer service and final delivery. In the second phase of business, we are going to hire as per the below strategy:

- A full time production assistant: Support photo and video shooting. The candidates for this will come from President's experience with freelancers

- A full time editor: Support photo editing, photo printing, web uploading, YouTube, etc.
- A business manager to assist with the sales and invoicing process
- Temporary need and project based staffing by leveraging freelancers (Freelancers.com, craigslist.com)

Financial Plan

Forecast

Key Assumptions

- **Customers & Revenue:** We expect to serve an average of 700 customers per annum, primarily in photoshoot projects, during year 1 and then increase that exponentially from year 2 through marketing and business development activities
- **Profit Margin:** We expect a 25% profit margin, with logistics, print, insurance and infrastructure to be the major overhead expenses
- **Marketing:** We will have a modest advertising budget as most of the marketing will be through search engine optimization.
- **People:** The first-year people costs will be minimal as we intend to use services / people on sites such as Freelancers or Craigslist, who would be able to support the volumes of work that we envisage. As things ramp up, we will bring on a couple of employees to assist.
- **Investments:** We forecast slow business in the initial months. Initial investments may need to be relatively high. By focusing on customer delight and high quality solutions, we will arrive at a suitable mix of demand vs supply which will recover our investments

Revenue by Month

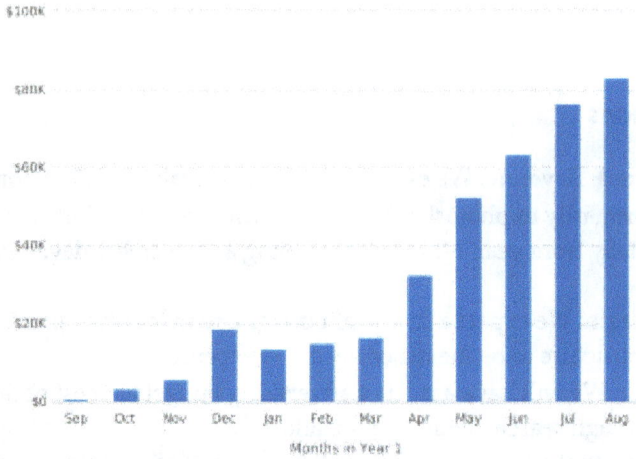

Expenses by Month

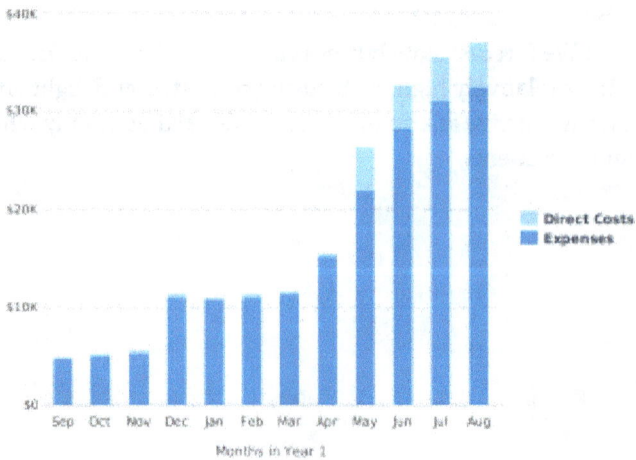

Net Profit (or Loss) by Year

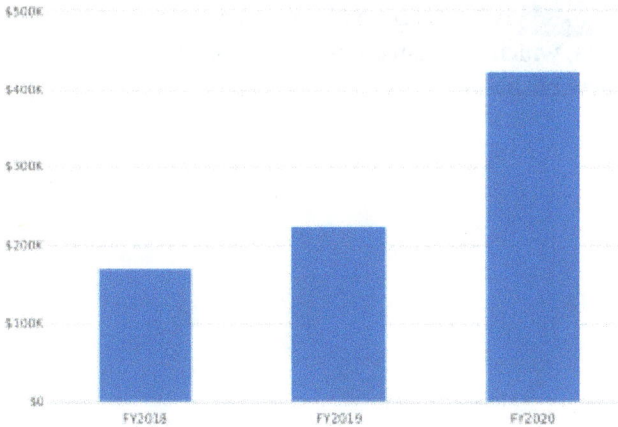

Financing

Use of Funds

- Costs in Year 1:
  - Primary use of our funds will be for cameras, lenses, lighting equipment, drones, large format printers, editing software/hardware, followed by logistics, print, insurance and infrastructure
  - Payroll cost: The first-year payroll costs will be kept minimal by leveraging temporary staffing and freelancers from Freelancers or Craigslist. Additionally, we will prefer to work on a cost per unit model which will help optimize costs.
- Costs in Year 2:
  - Payroll costs: Hiring design and sales employees and redirect effort of our President to business development, marketing and expansion programs
  - Advertising budget
  - Maintenance and repair / replacement budget will increase slightly for equipment

Sources of Funds

- The ███████████ is 100% funded by the parent company in Argentia, San Juan Cinema Ltda, which liquidated one of its properties in Argentia to help kick start this new business

Statements

Projected Profit & Loss

	FY2018	FY2019	FY2020
Revenue	$380,000	$700,000	$1,000,000
Direct Costs	$19,900	$142,215	$187,987
Gross Margin	$360,100	$557,785	$812,013
Gross Margin %	95%	80%	81%
Operating Expenses			
Salary	$60,000	$142,800	$154,560
Employee Related Expenses	$7,200	$17,136	$18,547
Rent	$4,980	$7,500	$9,000
Marketing	$9,500	$17,500	$25,000
Maintenance	$9,218	$21,000	$30,000
Fees	$2,400	$2,400	$2,400
Utilities	$15,200	$28,000	$40,000
Stationery	$11,400	$21,000	$30,000
Telecommunication	$12,000	$12,000	$12,000
Transportation	$18,000	$18,000	$18,000
Total Operating Expenses	$149,898	$287,336	$339,507
Operating Income	$210,203	$270,449	$472,505
Interest Incurred			
Depreciation and Amortization	$20,000	$20,000	$18,333
Income Taxes	$19,020	$25,045	$47,051
Total Expenses	$208,818	$474,596	$576,545
Net Profit	$171,182	$225,404	$423,455
Net Profit / Sales	45%	32%	42%

Projected Balance Sheet

	FY2018	FY2019	FY2020
Cash	$244,015	$477,619	$935,798
Accounts Receivable	$0	$0	$0
Inventory			
Other Current Assets			
Total Current Assets	**$244,015**	**$477,619**	**$935,798**
Long-Term Assets	$60,000	$60,000	
Accumulated Depreciation	($20,000)	($40,000)	
Total Long-Term Assets	**$40,000**	**$20,000**	
Total Assets	**$284,015**	**$497,619**	**$935,798**
Accounts Payable	$7,045	$5,536	$7,477
Income Taxes Payable	$12,988	$6,377	$13,200
Sales Taxes Payable	$17,800	$14,120	$20,080
Short-Term Debt			
Prepaid Revenue			
Total Current Liabilities	**$37,833**	**$26,033**	**$40,757**
Long-Term Debt			
Total Liabilities	**$37,833**	**$26,033**	**$40,757**
Paid-in Capital	$75,000	$75,000	$75,000
Retained Earnings		$171,182	$396,586
Earnings	$171,182	$225,404	$423,455
Total Owner's Equity	**$246,182**	**$471,586**	**$895,041**
Total Liabilities & Equity	**$284,015**	**$497,619**	**$935,798**

Projected Cash Flow Statement

	FY2018	FY2019	FY2020
Net Cash Flow from Operations			
Net Profit	$171,182	$225,404	$423,455
Depreciation and Amortization	$20,000	$20,000	$18,333
Change in Accounts Receivable	$0	$0	$0
Change in Inventory			
Change in Accounts Payable	$7,045	($1,509)	$1,941
Change in Income Tax Payable	$12,988	($6,611)	$6,823
Change in Sales Tax Payable	$17,800	($3,680)	$5,960
Change in Prepaid Revenue			
Net Cash Flow from Operations	**$229,015**	**$233,604**	**$440,179**
Investing & Financing			
Assets Purchased or Sold	($60,000)		$18,000
Investments Received	$75,000		
Change in Long-Term Debt			
Change in Short-Term Debt			
Dividends & Distributions			
Net Cash Flow from Investing & Financing	**$15,000**		**$18,000**
Cash at Beginning of Period	$0	$244,015	$477,619
Net Change in Cash	$244,015	$233,604	$458,179
Cash at End of Period	**$244,015**	**$477,619**	**$935,798**

Appendix

Profit and Loss Statement

Profit and Loss Statement (With Monthly Detail)

FY2018	Sep '17	Oct '17	Nov '17	Dec '17	Jan '18	Feb '18	Mar '18	Apr '18	May '18	Jun '18	Jul '18	Aug '18
Revenue	$500	$3,250	$5,500	$18,500	$13,500	$15,000	$16,500	$32,500	$52,250	$63,250	$76,250	$80,000
Direct Costs	$0	$150	$300	$300	$300	$300	$300	$300	$4,450	$4,450	$4,450	$4,600
Gross Margin	$500	$3,100	$5,200	$18,200	$13,200	$14,700	$16,200	$32,200	$47,800	$58,800	$71,800	$75,400
Gross Margin %	100%	95%	95%	98%	98%	98%	98%	99%	91%	93%	94%	94%
Operating Expenses												
Salary				$4,000	$4,000	$4,000	$4,000	$4,000	$7,000	$11,000	$11,000	$11,000
Employee Related Expenses				$400	$400	$400	$400	$400	$840	$1,320	$1,320	$1,320
Rent	$415	$415	$415	$415	$415	$415	$415	$415	$415	$415	$415	$415
Marketing	$13	$81	$137	$163	$237	$375	$413	$812	$1,307	$1,581	$1,936	$2,075
Maintenance								$975	$1,568	$1,897	$2,218	$2,480
Fees	$200	$200	$200	$200	$200	$200	$200	$200	$200	$200	$200	$200
Utilities	$20	$130	$220	$740	$840	$900	$960	$1,300	$2,000	$2,530	$3,050	$3,320
Stationery	$15	$96	$163	$255	$405	$450	$485	$975	$1,567	$1,898	$2,167	$2,480
Telecommunication	$1,000	$1,000	$1,000	$1,000	$1,000	$1,000	$1,000	$1,000	$1,000	$1,000	$1,000	$1,000
Transportation	$1,500	$1,500	$1,500	$1,500	$1,500	$1,500	$1,500	$1,500	$1,500	$1,500	$1,500	$1,500

The ▉▉▉▉

Total Operating Expenses	$3,163	$3,423	$3,638	$9,352	$8,878	$9,030	$9,162	$11,658	$17,486	$23,341	$24,967	$25,890
Operating Income	($3,663)	($323)	$1,562	$8,848	$4,322	$5,680	$7,838	$30,542	$30,314	$35,459	$46,834	$52,590
Interest Incurred												
Depreciation and Amortization	$1,667	$1,666	$1,667	$1,667	$1,666	$1,667	$1,667	$1,666	$1,667	$1,667	$1,666	$1,667
Income Taxes	$0	$0	$0	$76	$365	$642	$837	$3,887	$2,885	$3,379	$4,517	$5,092
Total Expenses	$4,829	$5,341	$5,604	$11,395	$11,109	$11,389	$11,666	$15,511	$26,468	$32,837	$35,600	$37,169
Net Profit	($4,329)	($1,991)	($104)	$7,105	$2,391	$3,611	$4,834	$16,909	$25,782	$30,413	$40,650	$45,831
Net Profit / Sales	(866%)	(61%)	(2%)	38%	18%	24%	29%	52%	49%	48%	53%	55%

The █████████

	FY2018	FY2019	FY20█
Revenue	$380,000	$700,000	$1,000,0█
Direct Costs	$19,900	$142,215	$187,9█
Gross Margin	$360,100	$957,785	$812,0█
Gross Margin %	95%	80%	8█
Operating Expenses			
Salary	$60,000	$142,000	$164,5█
Employee Related Expenses	$7,200	$17,126	$18,5█
Rent	$4,900	$7,500	$9,0█
Marketing	$9,500	$17,500	$25,0█
Maintenance	$9,218	$25,000	$30,0█
Fees	$2,400	$2,400	$2,4█
Utilities	$16,200	$28,000	$40,0█
Stationery	$11,400	$20,000	$30,0█
Telecommunication	$12,000	$12,000	$12,0█
Transportation	$18,000	$18,000	$18,0█
Total Operating Expenses	$149,898	$287,336	$339,50█
Operating Income	$210,203	$270,449	$472,50█
Interest Incurred			
Depreciation and Amortization	$28,000	$28,000	$18,33█
Income Taxes	$18,020	$25,045	$47,0█
Total Expenses	$208,818	$474,596	$576,54█
Net Profit	$171,182	$225,404	$423,45█

The ▮▮▮▮▮

Net Profit / Sales	45%	32%	42%

Balance Sheet

Balance Sheet (With Monthly Detail)

FY2018	Sep '17	Oct '17	Nov '17	Dec '17	Jan '18	Feb '18	Mar '18	Apr '18	May '18	Jun '18	Jul '18	Aug '18
Cash	$13,959	$14,101	$16,285	$26,490	$31,655	$38,606	$42,532	$66,922	$102,725	$130,542	$184,289	$244,016
Accounts Receivable	$0	$0	$0	$0	$0	$0	$0	$0	$0	$0	$0	$0
Inventory												
Other Current Assets												
Total Current Assets	$13,959	$14,101	$16,285	$26,490	$31,655	$38,606	$42,532	$66,922	$102,725	$130,542	$184,289	$244,016
Long-Term Assets	$60,000	$60,000	$60,000	$60,000	$60,000	$60,000	$60,000	$60,000	$60,000	$60,000	$60,000	$60,000
Accumulated Depreciation	($1,667)	($3,333)	($5,000)	($6,667)	($8,333)	($10,000)	($11,667)	($13,333)	($15,000)	($16,667)	($18,333)	($20,000)
Total Long-Term Assets	$58,333	$56,667	$55,000	$53,333	$51,667	$50,000	$48,333	$46,667	$45,000	$43,333	$41,667	$40,000
Total Assets	$72,292	$70,767	$71,285	$79,823	$83,322	$88,606	$90,865	$113,589	$147,725	$173,876	$225,955	$284,016
Accounts Payable	$1,581	$1,787	$1,969	$2,516	$2,349	$2,428	$2,441	$3,739	$5,648	$5,736	$6,548	$7,645
Income Taxes Payable	$0	$0	$0	$76	$341	$743	$537	$2,424	$5,249	$3,379	$7,896	$12,588
Sales Taxes Payable	$40	$300	$740	$1,480	$2,560	$3,740	$1,370	$3,920	$8,190	$5,060	$11,160	$17,600
Short-Term Debt												
Prepaid Revenue												
Total Current Liabilities	$1,621	$2,087	$2,709	$4,142	$5,250	$6,923	$4,348	$10,083	$18,437	$14,175	$25,604	$37,833

Debt

$1,621	$2,087	$2,709	$4,142	$5,250	$6,923	$4,348	$10,063	$18,437	$14,175	$25,604	$37,833
$75,000	$75,000	$75,000	$75,000	$75,000	$75,000	$75,000	$75,000	$75,000	$75,000	$75,000	$75,000
($4,329)	($6,320)	($6,434)	$481	$3,072	$6,683	$11,517	$28,506	$54,288	$84,701	$125,351	$171,182
$70,671	$68,680	$68,576	$75,681	$78,072	$81,683	$86,517	$103,506	$129,288	$159,701	$200,351	$246,182
$72,292	$70,767	$71,285	$79,823	$83,322	$88,606	$90,865	$113,589	$147,725	$173,876	$225,955	$284,015

	FY2018	FY2019	FY2020
Cash	$244,015	$477,619	$935,798
Accounts Receivable	$0	$0	$0
Inventory			
Other Current Assets			
Total Current Assets	$244,015	$477,619	$935,798
Long-Term Assets	$60,000	$60,000	
Accumulated Depreciation	($20,000)	($40,000)	
Total Long-Term Assets	$40,000	$20,000	
Total Assets	$284,015	$497,619	$935,798
Accounts Payable	$7,045	$5,526	$7,477
Income Taxes Payable	$13,988	$6,377	$13,280
Sales Taxes Payable	$17,800	$14,130	$20,000
Short-Term Debt			
Prepaid Revenue			
Total Current Liabilities	$37,833	$26,033	$40,757
Long-Term Debt			
Total Liabilities	$37,833	$26,033	$40,757
Paid-in Capital	$75,000	$75,000	$75,000
Retained Earnings		$171,182	$396,586
Earnings	$171,182	$225,404	$423,455
Total Owner's Equity	$246,182	$471,586	$895,041
Total Liabilities & Equity	$284,015	$497,619	$935,798

sh Flow Statement

h Flow Statement (With Monthly Detail)

	Sep '17	Oct '17	Nov '17	Dec '17	Jan '18	Feb '18	Mar '18	Apr '18	May '18	Jun '18	Jul '18	Aug '18
sh Flow												
tions												
rofit	($4,329)	($1,991)	($904)	$7,105	$2,391	$3,611	$4,834	$16,989	$25,782	$30,413	$40,650	$45,831
eciative tization	$1,667	$1,667	$1,667	$1,667	$1,667	$1,667	$1,667	$1,667	$1,667	$1,667	$1,667	$1,667
ge in unts vable	$0	$0	$0	$0	$0	$0	$0	$0	$0	$0	$0	$0
ge in tary												
ge in unts ble	$1,591	$306	$182	$418	($230)	$71	$71	$1,248	$1,309	$688	$813	$497
ge in me Tax ble	$0	$0	$0	$76	$265	$402	($206)	$1,817	$2,865	($1,900)	$4,517	$5,092
ge in Sales Payable	$40	$360	$440	$740	$1,080	$1,320	($2,440)	$2,620	$4,180	($3,040)	$6,100	$6,640
ge in aid sue												
sh Flow ations	($1,041)	$142	$2,194	$10,205	$5,165	$6,951	$3,936	$24,390	$35,803	$27,817	$53,746	$59,727
ting & cing												

Assets Purchased or Sold	(\$60,000)											
Investments Received	\$75,000											
Change In Long-Term Debt												
Change In Short-Term Debt												
Dividends & Distributions												
Net Cash Flow from Investing & Financing	**\$15,000**											
Cash at Beginning of Period	\$0	\$13,959	\$14,101	\$16,285	\$26,490	\$31,655	\$38,606	\$42,532	\$66,922	\$102,725	\$130,542	\$184,289
Net Change in Cash	\$13,959	\$142	\$2,184	\$10,205	\$5,165	\$6,951	\$3,926	\$24,390	\$35,803	\$27,817	\$53,746	\$59,727
Cash at End of Period	**\$13,959**	**\$14,101**	**\$16,285**	**\$26,490**	**\$31,655**	**\$38,606**	**\$42,532**	**\$66,922**	**\$102,725**	**\$130,542**	**\$184,289**	**\$244,016**

	FY2018	FY2019	FY2020
Net Cash Flow from Operations			
Net Profit	$171,182	$225,404	$423,405
Depreciation and Amortization	$30,000	$33,000	$18,333
Change in Accounts Receivable	$0	$0	$0
Change in Inventory			
Change in Accounts Payable	$7,045	($1,500)	$1,941
Change in Income Tax Payable	$12,988	($5,611)	$5,023
Change in Sales Tax Payable	$17,800	($3,600)	$5,900
Change in Prepaid Revenue			
Net Cash Flow from Operations	**$229,015**	**$233,604**	**$440,579**
Investing & Financing			
Assets Purchased or Sold	($60,000)		$18,000
Investments Received	$75,000		
Change in Long-Term Debt			
Change in Short-Term Debt			
Dividends & Distributions			
Net Cash Flow from Investing & Financing	**$15,000**		**$18,000**
Cash at Beginning of Period	$0	$244,015	$477,619
Net Change in Cash	$244,015	$233,604	$458,579
Cash at End of Period	**$244,015**	**$477,619**	**$936,798**

www.ingramcontent.com/pod-product-compliance
Lightning Source LLC
Chambersburg PA
CBHW070808300326
41914CB00078B/1900/J